FEELING HAPPY, FEELING STRONG

Exercises for Transforming Stress, Anxiety, Worry and Fear into Deeper Connection with Ourselves

Suzanne Wylde

Many Trees Publishing

Copyright © 2020 Suzanne Wylde

All rights reserved. The moral rights of the author have been asserted. No part of this book may be reproduced or used in any manner without written permission of the copyright owner except for the use of quotations in a book review.

FIRST EDITION

www.suzannewylde.com

This book is not intended as a substitute for the medical advice of physicians, mental health professionals or for medication. If you require assistance contact a licenced professional or relevant organisation.

Although the author has made every effort to ensure that the information in this book was correct at press time, the author does not assume and hereby disclaims any liability to any party for any loss, damage, or disruption caused by errors or omissions, whether such errors or omissions result from negligence, accident, or any other cause.

Cover design: graphictional

*Thanks to difficult situations for making me stronger.
Thanks to really, really difficult situations for making
me much stronger.*

*And thank you to all the people who have
taught me how to convert this painful
challenge into growth and resilience.*

CONTENTS

Title Page
Copyright
Dedication
Preface   1
Introduction   3
Chapter 1: Getting Back into our Body   7
Chapter 2: Accepting Ourselves and Our   14
Emotions
Chapter 3: Working With Our Feelings   24
Chapter 4: Reconnecting with Reality   30
Chapter 5: Behaving Like Yourself and   36
Thinking and Acting Clearly
Chapter 6: A Little More Information   44
Conclusion   60
Appendix: The Exercises   62
Praise For Author   79

Books By This Author

PREFACE

Right now I am at home, as most of the nation is and many other nations around the globe are. I am lucky that I am a writer and I can occupy myself with that, whereas usually I fit my square-eyed scribbling around working with clients. Like many people I feel a need to offer what support I can, even if that is just a little. So I have written this brief guide in the hope that it may help some people struggling with stronger-than-usual emotions of fear, anxiety, stress, worry and other feelings resulting from loss of control or a sense of powerlessness.

In times of uncertainty and upheaval we can face a mixture of strong and sometimes unfamiliar emotions. This can be especially tricky if we have never been taught how to work through these feelings in a conscious way and we can feel overwhelmed as if by formidable and invisible forces.

I want to teach you some simple tools to use so that even in the hardest times you can regain your footing and act effectively and authentically. Many people are saying that the way we act now will be remembered for years to come, will be a reflection of our character and integrity.

As I sit here the sun beams down on the garden outside releasing the lively smells of spring and as always it brings back strong memories of childhood. When the classroom windows were opened for the first time that year and the lazy hum of lawn mowers carried my mind away from the teacher's voice as if it was floating on the warm spring breeze. It all seems so at odds with the seriousness of current events.

But that is life; good and bad, easy and hard. And when it is really hard the good is even better, that is our compensation. So I suggest trying to work through the difficult emotions when they come up and enjoy the good ones while they last, acting within our integrity and looking forward to a future that is easier because of our newfound strength.

INTRODUCTION

This is a very short book. I wanted to get the essentials down so that people can start using the exercises and benefitting from them, so unlike my other (longer) books it is not meticulously researched and does not cover lots of theory. Instead I have focused on giving you the most effective tools that I have seen work with my clients.

When we feel stressed, anxious or fearful it can be hard to take in a lot of information. In this state it is easier to take in small parcels of information, so this guide is broken up into bite-sized chunks.

I have also used quite simple language to keep it easy to digest. For example, a textbook would not use the words "feeling" and "emotion" interchangeably as I have here (it would probably also not mention "dancing unicorns" - you have been forewarned).

In addition, most self-respecting books would not lump fear, anxiety, worry and stress all in together. Because I have seen how these feelings are often interwoven and meshed together in my work with clients, this is a guide to dealing with these kinds of feelings rather picking out just one to deal with in isolation.

Because this is an experiential guide, as you read it it walks you through a process. If you are in a public place or do not feel like doing the exercises you can skip over them and come back to them later. However, since this book is intended to help you get a certain result I highly recommend you wait until you are ready to do the practical steps at the same time.

As you go through there will be bits of information alternating with exercises. If a concept is unfamiliar, you can take some time to consider it before moving on. The exercises may also be quite new to you so take your time.

If an exercise is challenging that is actually a good sign – the areas that are hardest to work on often hold the greatest benefit. Try not to be self-critical; it is fine to try again later and as many times as you like. If an exercise seems silly I want to encourage you that I have included it because I have seen it work for people. A lot of this work is about getting out of your head and sometimes being silly or doing something outside of your ordinary behaviour is an effective way to do that.

I am not a counsellor, but I think they're great – if you feel you need one you should definitely find one you resonate with, or contact an organisation that can help you.

My background is fairly eclectic: I am a Traditional Chinese medicine practitioner, stretching trainer, energy worker, holistic coach and author. I work with people physically to improve their posture, health and wellbeing and I also help people with their self-development work to help them express more of themselves and move past stubborn obstacles.

My self-development journey has been fairly colourful so far. I do experience all of the emotions this book focuses on, as everyone does. And I use the exercises in this book myself, as I have also coached many clients to do.

I have included all the things that I have found to work, but they may not all work for you. I recommend choosing the exercises that are the most effective and making them a part of your daily (or at least weekly) life. I have also put some resources that you will find useful for this book on my site here: https://www.suzannewylde.com/happyandstrong.

As you progress through the book you may feel like repeating one of the earlier exercises again, which is absolutely fine. I have laid the exercises out in the order I think is most suitable, but if your intuition tells you to do it differently, I would listen to that impulse. All of the exercises are listed together at the end so you can find them easily when you want to revisit them.

If an exercise intensifies your feelings too much or you feel overwhelmed, take a break and try one that makes you feel more grounded. You can revisit a challenging exercise when you are feeling more centred. Other ways to "water down" an exercise that feels too strong are: not breathing as deeply, keeping your eyes open where it says to close them and doing it for a much shorter time. Be kind to yourself and only do what feels good and manageable.

Also, if a certain exercise is not manageable for you physically you can either modify it to something you can do or visualise doing it, which also holds a lot of benefits. For example, if you have a disability and cannot wiggle your feet you can wiggle something else or you can imagine wiggling them. Either way some form of wiggling is great.

In this book we are going to focus on bringing you back into your body, increasing self-awareness, learning to intentionally work with your emotions and hear what they are saying and become more and more grounded in reality. A lot of this work is about being intentional, embodied and having a relationship with the parts of you that feel scared.

Let's get started!

CHAPTER 1: GETTING BACK INTO OUR BODY

How are you feeling right now?

Just have a quick think – don't deliberate for too long.

Now have a big yawn and stretch. And then exaggerate it, open your mouth really wide and make a sound as you sigh or yawn loudly. Repeat this as you move your body a little more in the way that feels good to you.

How are you feeling now?

Because our emotions affect our whole body, changing our physical state can break us out of an unhelpful feedback loop. So when our mind and body are telling each other we should feel anxious or fearful and they keep reinforcing that message to each other, it is helpful to know how to step in and interrupt that cycle.

But more than that, we need to connect to our

body because it is our foundation. A strong connection can help us to feel at home in ourselves, comfy, grounded, self-assured and settled in, while a weaker connection can make us feel restless, unrooted, ungrounded or lacking in self-confidence.

Many of us float up into the top of our heads like a balloon bobbing in the breeze - the overthinking of an intellectual society can fill us with helium in this way (metaphorically speaking). Pulling ourselves back down into our body, feeling our physical sensations and listening to them, loving our body, moving it and enjoying it can allow us to be fully alive in the moment. On the other hand, living mainly in our head stops us from feeling and connecting to others fully.

> Bearing this in mind (no pun intended), have another powerful yawn and stretch, really feeling the strength and other sensations in your body

It is not just the helium of intellectual societies that pulls us up into our heads, we can be chased up out of our bodies by fear. But, you may think, how can that be when my body is having such a strong physical response to my feelings of fear or anxiety? Often your body has those feelings on a kind of autopilot while you get caught up in the feelings in a disconnected and ungrounded way. When anxious or fearful emotions dominate it is hard for us to be fully aware of our bodies and connected to them.

This makes total sense when you consider that you don't want to be overwhelmed by your emotions in moments of danger. So not feeling a lot of physical sensations (which communicate our emotions to us) may be an evolutionary advantage.

However, in the long term we need to feel our feelings and physical sensations to be fully alive. And since we are having emotions and they are affecting us either way – we may as well feel them properly.

Let's get a little more in touch with our body now, and really settle in.

Coming Back into Your Body

As you do this exercise either choose the option that applies to you the most or make another one up that feels true. Also, try to look either straight ahead or down, but not up.

Put your hands on your belly

Look down at your body and say "hello body, thank you for _____ [moving me around/ making life enjoyable/ working hard/ digesting all my food/ keeping me going/ storing all my feelings and other aspects of me]. I love you, thank you".

Now rub your hands up and down your

thighs strongly, bringing your awareness
into the feeling in your legs.

Wiggle your toes and circle your feet around,
bringing that awareness into your lower legs also.

When you feel that you are very connected to
your legs, expand that awareness from your legs
through your hips and then to your whole torso
and your arms. As you do this you can also move
and breathe in the way you feel your body wants to
in order to get that awareness everywhere in your
body (safely and without pain) for as long as you
feel like. Groaning or yawning noises may help.

What does it feel like to be more connected
to your body right now?

Stay with this feeling as you take
a deep breath in and out

See if you can feel this feeling even more fully
as you take another breath in and out

Did you feel more; empowered, calm, strong, grounded, centred or other? Take a moment to express how this made you feel (if positive) and then acknowledge that you now have the ability to get back into this feeling whenever you want to.

If you felt anything bad or difficult, that is OK – it

was in there anyway, you just became more aware of it. Becoming aware of difficult emotions makes it possible to work with them, so try to acknowledge these feelings as much as you can comfortably.

And if you found this exercise hard, don't worry - many of us find it difficult to fully inhabit and connect to our bodies. You can come back to it as many times as you like and each time will probably be a little easier.

Staying in your body can help you to: avoid getting caught up in worries and negative repetitive thoughts, avoid acting reactively, maintain healthy boundaries, stay in the moment, work through your feelings, be genuine, be loving and have more access to your mind.

Yes – strangely being all up in our head clouds our mind because we are not designed to work that way. Our mind and body have a synergistic relationship – being able to stomp around in the full extent of us, including our body, gives our mind room to work.

Or, to use a metaphor, a café full to the brim with coffee will not be able to make any coffee at all and also all the customers and staff will just be swimming about it in and possibly be very hyper.

Similarly, if we are completely up in our heads we will just be swirled about by random thoughts and thinking habits we have very little control over, and also sometimes feel quite hyper. The body brings us back into a liveable speed, grounds our thoughts into reality and reminds us that we are not information-processing robots.

Other things that can help us reconnect with our bodies (as long as we are not too much in our heads while doing them) include: exercise (where we are listening to our bodies, not just bossing them about), things that stimulate our senses, getting a massage, self-massage or having a bath, dancing, sex and other physical forms of self-expression.

If you have a difficult time staying in your body with one of these methods, just try a different one for a while. Some of us have had a tough time in life and this can make inhabiting our body fully feel difficult or even confronting. If this is the case for you then go at a rate that feels safe and sustainable. You might also think about finding a pro like a counsellor to help with that as they have experience of guiding people back into their bodies.

You are doing great so far, well done!

As a nice way to end the chapter and the furthest from being up in our heads that I could think of, let's give ourselves a foot massage.

Why?

It feels good.

Also, there is also almost nothing that signals "I am not in danger" to our bodies, hearts and minds than taking the time to massage our feet.

So pop one foot up and gently work into those muscles. You can also circle your foot around and then gently stretch your toes back and forth with your hands.

Without causing any pain, increase the firmness so you are releasing tension you do not need, but in a smooth and flowing way so your feet feel reassured.

Yes, feet can feel reassured.

Take a deep, slow and relaxing breath, yawn and stretch if you feel like it.

I hope you are starting to feel more reassured too. If not, don't worry, there's still plenty of book left.

CHAPTER 2: ACCEPTING OURSELVES AND OUR EMOTIONS

Accepting all aspects of ourselves (including our emotions, mind, body, personality and other bits) is important for dealing with fearful and anxious feelings. This is because acceptance makes us feel safe and feeling safe allows us to work through these emotions.

It also keeps us in our bodies, as well as centred and open-minded. So, while fear and anxiety often create a state of being closed-down, stuck or rigid, self-acceptance can foster a state of openness and flexibility.

> *"Tension is who you think you should be. Relaxation is who you are."*
>
> —Chinese proverb

The open and healthy playing field that self-acceptance creates is really great for this work. If it does not feel natural that's totally fine, it is something we can work towards with practice. But you absolutely deserve the self-regard and the spaciousness that comes with it.

Taking a Moment to Fully Recognise How Well You Are Doing

In this exercise we are going to say a short phrase to ourselves to acknowledge our worth and to feel self-acceptance and self-love. If the phrase seems too much or wrong you can change it – as long as it is still positive.

Close your eyes, breathe deeply and in a relaxed way

> Let a feeling of warmth and love grow in your chest and spread throughout your body

> Say to yourself "*I am good, I am strong, I am enough*" and breathe in and out slowly and deeply

> If anything comes up to block that, just accept that part of you, whilst also knowing you can feel a level of self-love and self-acceptance at the same time – there is space for both within you.

> Repeat the phrase "*I am good, I am strong, I am enough*" the number of times that feels right

Let the feeling of warmth, self-acceptance and self-love move around your body anywhere it is needed. It can even encompass difficult emotions or areas of your body you have a hard time loving

When you are ready to end the exercise take a deep breath in and out and open your eyes

If that was difficult, it is a great sign that this may be a growth area for you. Accepting the resistance that comes up (for example if your mind reacts by thinking "this is stupid/ this writer is clearly crazy/ but I am not enough!") and encompassing that resistance with feelings of self-love and self-acceptance is more helpful than trying to fight against it.

Resistance is OK, a part of you is just scared – love and accept that part that is trying to keep you safe.

You are doing really well.

Feel that compliment in your body.

Accepting Our Bodies

Self-acceptance and being connected to our body are very interconnected, maybe because they both bring us closer to the core of ourselves. If we accept our body just the way it is, we are using a mixture of these two qualities.

Just like a toddler who stands proudly displaying her large tummy for the whole world to admire without any doubt of her worth, fully accepting ourselves brings us home, to the truth that we are perfect the way we are right now.

Accepting my Body

Take a deep breath in and out slowly.

Put your hands on your body wherever you like – chest, shoulders, stomach, legs.

Say in your mind or aloud: "this is my perfect body" (and if you feel that your body is not perfect right now for some reason add the phrase "thank you for doing your best for me".)

If that is hard, just accept the feeling of it being hard and feel good about your effort, then try it again.

Take another deep breath in and out.

Great job embodied person, and great tummy!

Accepting your body and inhabiting it fully not only helps you to feel safe enough to process fear and anxiety – it also allows you to access more of your personal power. Feeling centred in your genuine power naturally deflects unnecessary fear. And if fear is relevant and proportional, staying in your power will help you to see the situation more clearly and take action if needed.

So, self-love, being embodied, being present, standing in our power and accepting ourselves and our feelings are all inextricably connected. Working on one will often benefit the others.

Let's move on now to accepting our feelings.

Accepting Our Feelings

As we start to work with our emotions it is good to know that although we are aiming for complete acceptance, we do not have to be perfect at it. So, as you work through this part remember to be kind to yourself.

Ideally we want to accept our full range of emotions and the fact that we are emotional beings who have feelings even if our minds deem them irrational or if we find them uncomfortable.

Of course, some emotions are easier for us to feel and others are a little harder to stomach. If we want to stay grounded and have a lot of access to different parts of ourselves then the more feelings we can accept and feel, the better.

Aside from the fact that acceptance lets us see our emotions in the first place, it is also particularly important for helping our feelings feel safe enough to open up and for giving them the space they need to express themselves.

When we reject a feeling it is usually pushed down or squashed into a confined space within us. Trying to work with them in that state is pretty impossible. Luckily, feeling our emotions and accepting them is something that we can learn and improve at through practice.

It is also easy to get caught up in a state and not know how to get out of it and to judge ourselves for that. Common thoughts such as; "I should be able to control my feelings" or "well, other people are starving/out of work/ in a much worse situation, so I should feel OK by comparison" may be an attempt to rationalise ourselves out of the feeling.

If that worked we would probably be feeling a lot less anxious or afraid, but unfortunately it does not.

However, in our intellectual society it makes perfect sense that we would try and think our way out of a feeling state.

> Let's take a moment and remember that
> it is OK that we are not perfect.

<u>Taking a Moment to Remember That We're Only Human</u>

Sit comfortably, put your hands on your heart, belly or legs, take a deep breath in and say "I accept that I am only human and I am doing the best I can"

Say it a few times if you want to, and after each time breathe in and feel that you are breathing in self-acceptance.

Be with the stillness that arises

Well done.

And now let's move on to accepting different kinds of emotions. In this relaxed exercise I am just going to mention some emotions for you to practice feeling acceptance of. If there are any missing that you particularly want to work with feel free to add them.

As you do this you do not need to feel the actual emotion, just the acceptance of it, while staying connected to your body. If one is difficult, there is no need to struggle, just make a mental note of it as an interesting fact and move on.

Try to be kind and non-judgemental towards yourself. This exercise is not meant to be stressful or triggering, but within your comfort zone and interesting. So, if you feel it is too challenging right now come back to it later.

Accepting a Wide Range of Emotions

Take a slow and relaxing breath in and out.

Be aware of your physical sensations
and accept anything you feel.

Going at your own pace, call to mind each of
the emotions below one at a time and feel your
acceptance of that emotion in your body. If it helps
you can think or say "I accept feeling___" for each.

If you find it hard to accept any, that is OK,
just accept that resistance and move on.

*Happy, annoyed, angry, weak, powerful, wrong,
embarrassed, anxious, excited, afraid, satisfied,
insecure, out-of-control, empowered*

Take a deep breath in and out

This exercise is about expanding to embrace all of our emotions and understanding a little bit more about our relationship to them. Of course working with the idea of an emotion is different to being right in the middle of it, and there are so many other emotions in addition to these, but this is still a great start.

It is also a good opportunity to spot any emotions we feel strong resistance to. If there are any that is useful for us to know. Remember this is not a fight, but a journey towards collaboration.

With practice you will be able to accept the emotion while still being fully in your body, accepting yourself as you are and being present. This will give you a lot more autonomy and control in terms of how you feel and live.

It may seem counterintuitive that accepting difficult emotions helps us. Surely, you may think - that will either increase those feelings or prevent a change in them?

Actually, acceptance means seeing them as they truly are and giving them a chance to express themselves, which can often lead to valuable insights and often resolution of these feelings.

Occasionally being fully aware of a feeling can make us feel overwhelmed, in which case we can switch our focus back to self-acceptance and coming back into the body. Although in the long-term being able to embrace these difficult emotions is essential for fully working through them, the pace that works best is our natural pace.

So be kind to yourself, keep breathing and keep connecting to your body and remember that you are perfect as you are and there is no rush.

CHAPTER 3: WORKING WITH OUR FEELINGS

Learning to process emotions is not like being a hunter who tracks them down and slays them. We could slay all day – it won't help. We don't actually want to fight them because they are a part of us that is trying to be heard. Therefore, struggling with our feelings, pushing them down or trying to get rid of them is like arm wrestling ourselves or punching ourselves in the face and then wondering why we don't feel better.

We have to learn to be with them, in a non-judgemental way, in a *non-problem-solving* way - as friendly equals who want to understand each other.

To do that we need to get in touch with them and since all emotions announce themselves through physical sensations, we need to get fully down into our bodies to connect with them.

In the exercise we allow the feeling to show itself as a shape or object, which looks like a representation of it rather than a specific situation or part of your anatomy. For example, an ache in your muscle will not look like a picture of a muscle, but maybe a purple blob or a green triangle. Also, do not worry if the shape or sensation morphs through this process, just be with it and allow it to be what it wants to.

Let's have a go.

Connecting to Our Physical Sensations

(For this exercise only look straight ahead or down – but not up)

Go ahead and rub your thighs quite firmly again.

Have a move around of your body.

Have a yawn and a loud sigh.

Now pause and notice how your body is feeling. Are there any sensations at the forefront?

If there is nothing there right away, just be patient and breathe and relax as you wait.

Focus on the most noticeable feeling (or even an absence of feeling, such as numbness)

Describe it to yourself, possibly including temperature, colour, shape, feelings of heaviness/lightness or movement. Get as specific as you can.

When you have a complete picture in your mind, just put a pin in it for now and taking a deep breath, open your eyes

❖ ❖ ❖

Well done, this first important step can be hard if we are not used to tuning into our bodies and if it was tricky don't worry – it gets much easier with practice.

Now we are going to have a go at working with the feeling that came up (or if a different feeling becomes more noticeable you can work with that instead), starting with connecting to it through your physical sensations.

It is likely you will be speaking with a part of yourself so be kind.

<u>Connecting to Our Emotions and Working with Them</u>

Bring yourself fully into your body again
by rubbing your thighs, moving about a bit
and breathing deeply and slowly (while still
looking only ahead or down – not up).

Focus your awareness on your body and notice the
most obvious physical sensation. Just be aware of
it for a moment, without any need to do anything.

Holding it gently in your awareness, let a picture
form as if it was a representation of the feeling.
Allow all the details to appear including its: shape,
colour, temperature, texture or movement if any.

Once you have that pictured clearly in your mind, say "hello" to it and just be with it for a moment without expectation.

Then when you feel ready, ask it if it has anything it wants to say and wait for the answer with an open mind. There are no wrong answers, but we don't want our mind to step in and supply the answer, so try and just wait until something organically pops up.

If it answered you there is a chance that you could have a dialogue back and forth, so you can try that. If it did not answer you, that's fine, you can always try again at a later time.

Either way you can also ask "is there anything you want?"

If it answers, you can either have a dialogue with it, or just acknowledge its feelings.

When you feel that the conversation or interaction is complete you can end the exercise or you can repeat it with another noticeable physical sensation.

How did you get on? Focusing, staying with one feeling and listening with an open mind can all be tricky at the beginning. But not only does it get easier, you will be able to go deeper the more experienced you get.

Although this book is focusing on helping you work through feelings related to fear and anxiety, stay open to working with any emotion that comes up because they are all connected.

And, confusingly, other emotions that we are less comfortable feeling may get shunted into feelings of anxiety or fear, even if they are actually quite different emotions. Because emotions all have an energy and momentum of their own which has to go somewhere, they will often choose the path most travelled (aka a comfortably familiar feeling).

For example, a person who was brought up to repress anger may divert this red-faced and embarrassing emotion into a more socially-acceptable experience of anxiety or worry perhaps. And they will often do this reflexively without even knowing they have done it.

Unfortunately, anger is not usually resolved the same way that worry or anxiety is, so although this strategy is less uncomfortable in the short-term we can end up hanging onto that emotion that we didn't want to feel for a much longer time.

Therefore, by learning to accept all of our feelings we will have a greater ability to see them for what they are, listen to their message and let them move through us completely.

To further complicate matters, emotions often have other ones stuck to them like chewing gum on the sole of a shoe, or swirled throughout them like a raspberry ripple (fright and embarrassment perhaps? Not sure which emotion tastes the most like raspberry...).

Luckily, as I mentioned before, we do not need to untangle them in our minds – we can just work with the most obvious sensation and follow it wherever it leads.

I recommend you try doing this fairly regularly to start with, so that you get some practice. You should then find it easier and easier to tune in and hear what your emotions are saying.

OK, time for a yawn and stretch – make it big, make it loud and proud! Really go for the satisfaction.

Well done on what you have done so far!

CHAPTER 4: RECONNECTING WITH REALITY

You have already learned a lot of tools for working with fear and anxiety including; grounding yourself into your body, becoming more accepting of yourself, tuning into physical manifestations of emotions and then learning to talk to them.
What now?

Well, one of the big things that comes up with my clients time and time again is the need to re-connect powerfully with the reality of the situation. And anxiety, worry and fear can all knock us out of that, making it hard to think in proportion to what is actually going on or have a clear perspective.

Getting back to reality is easier when we are fully in our body, because bodies and the physical world are all about reality rather than abstract concepts. So, remember to ground yourself into your body, breathe deeply and descend down from your head when you feel caught up by a thought pattern or state that you are not in control of.

Practical Ways to Reconnect with Reality

Below are just a few ideas for ways to reconnect to reality, which all involve some kind of re-engagement with the physical world. They may not all work for you so just try and find the ones that work best.

Although our phones, computers, worries and repetitive thoughts may all attempt to draw our attention away, we are always right on top of the thing that is going to help us. The earth, nature and physicality – these are all an irrefutable part of our existence, and a part that makes things make sense.

So, while using one of the activities below, try to connect to your senses and feel how you are a part of the whole world, paying attention to how you are physically connected to it.

Ways to Reconnect with The Real World

Gardening (getting your hands and bare feet in the earth is great), walking, running or other exercise in nature, camping, building things, having a cup of tea in the garden, going up mountains, rolling down hills, swimming in lakes, rivers or the sea, relaxed surfing, bodyboarding, eating great food, going barefoot (where safe), spending time with animals, talking to plants, drumming and more.

Some things that seem really physical, but which are quite extreme can make us feel ungrounded and hyper, so I have not included things like skydiving or bungee jumping. However, they probably would make you forget your usual worries or fears!

The suggestions above are for dropping down into the pace of nature, fully inhabiting your body and feeling things more. So, although adrenaline sports can be great, they don't foster that kind of grounded calm that we are looking for in this work.

Ways to be Realistic in Our Thinking

In addition to being grounded in the reality of the physical world we also want to make sure our thoughts reflect the reality of any situation, thing or person they relate to. We all have stories we tell ourselves that are not strictly true, negative thoughts that repeat over and over, fear-based beliefs and other unhelpful mental patterns.

Taking the time to consciously examine the thoughts connected to the fear, worry or anxiety we are experiencing is valuable. If we are thinking something we want it to be real. Let's have a go at examining a couple of our fear-based thoughts or beliefs.

How Realistic Are Our Thoughts?

Identify one or two of these kinds of thoughts and then examine them thoroughly using the following questions. Try not to answer any reflexively, but take your time.

1. Is it absolutely true?

2. Would most other people agree with that thought or belief?

3. Is it in proportion? (e.g., being as terrified of making a spelling mistake as falling from a great height is out of proportion – even if you are a perfectionist)

4. If it is about yourself or another person, is it the most honest and loving it can be? Or is it unnecessarily harsh or critical?

If you have found that the thing or things you are thinking are not the most realistic or usefully kind, create the most real and useful version of them and write that down.

How does thinking that version of the thought feel?

In the future when you slip back into those repetitive and/or negative thoughts, you now know that you can step up as the leader of your mind, replacing incorrect or ungrounded thoughts with their more realistic counterpart.

You can be your own anchor.

Taking responsibility for maintaining a solid grip on reality is essential for being a mature, kind person. If our idea of reality is faulty then many actions (which would turn out great if our version of reality were true) backfire or have unexpected outcomes because they are not in line with the actual reality.

For example: let's say someone is worried that their boss does not like them, so they overcompensate and work way too much. However, their boss does not react gratefully, which reinforces the employee's belief that they are not liked and makes them worry even more.

Because the person's view of the situation lead them to act with ulterior motives (and these usually feel weird to people), getting the outcome they wanted with that attitude was unlikely.

If they had instead started by assessing their initial belief and taken a more realistic stance, they might have realised that their boss was most likely just busy and thinking about her own pressing concerns. The employee would have acted in a more natural way and potentially got a more satisfactory result.

But regardless of the result, they would have felt more grounded in themselves and better able to deal with whatever happened next.

So, it is often possible to cut a spiral into negativity off at the knees by looking at whether the underlying thoughts are based on the actual reality or not.

I also recommend that you challenge any negative thinking, curate your thoughts so they reflect your genuine personality and take the time to clean up your mind from time to time. A messy or unloved mind can lead to unnecessary self-doubt or fear, just as an ungrounded body can.

Being realistic also frees up a lot of energy and creates a much stronger position, which we can use for being a kind and useful person to others.

CHAPTER 5: BEHAVING LIKE YOURSELF AND THINKING AND ACTING CLEARLY

Some of us deal with stress better than others. I don't know about you but I can get critical or grumpy. If you know that some of your behaviour recently has not been ideal this chapter may be useful for you.

Take a moment and write down what that behaviour is specifically. Now, work backwards to try and identify what triggered that behaviour. When you have found the trigger consider why that might be.

For example: *"I feel grumpy towards my friend because an hour ago someone made me feel like I wasn't competent. That is hard for me because my sisters always told me I did things wrong and teased me, which made me feel hurt and anxious. I don't like feeling that way so I turn it into a bad mood instead, which feels easier to deal with and is also protective"*.

Below is an exercise for accepting that you have

acted in a way that was not quite right for you. Not accepting it intellectually, but emotionally. This acceptance will help you to move back towards a more authentic way of behaving.

Try to allow yourself to feel that acceptance in your heart as deeply as possible. This can be a challenge as some people do not like to admit they made a mistake and the feeling of that can be very hard. On the other hand, others of us do not like to let ourselves off the hook so easily.

I hear what you're saying. Try it anyway.

Accepting We Behaved Poorly

Write the sentence that sums up your behaviour the most accurately, choosing the right words for you, (they can be different to the examples given below):

"I accept that I was _____ [rude/ short/ passive aggressive/ critical/ stubborn/ angry] because I felt _____ [stressed/ afraid/ disrespected/ insecure/ unloved/ anxious]".

And then, with your hands on your heart, say in your mind or aloud:
"I accept that sometimes I get _____ when I feel ____"

Breathe in acceptance of that statement

Breathe out with a wide open mouth letting

> go of any need to be perfect
>
> Breathe in self-acceptance deeply
>
> Breathe out with a wide open mouth letting go of any self-imposed pressure
>
> (repeat until you feel finished)

Accepting that we acted badly is not saying that acting badly is OK - it is saying that it is OK that we are flawed. Accepting that and the reality of how we behaved will give us the space we need to change it. On the other hand, shame will back us into a corner and is more likely to lead to us behaving in the same way again. People who like themselves want to behave well.

Another key part of changing any behaviour that is outside of our integrity is to learn to notice what triggers it and then intentionally work through your feelings around that trigger.

For example, the trigger mentioned above was the person being told they were not competent. So to work on that, they would connect to their physical feelings while contemplating that trigger and then work through the feelings that arise (the exercise *"Connecting to Our Emotions and Working with Them"* is useful here).

We may or may not realise what the initial cause of that trigger was (e.g. above it was being teased in childhood), but either way we can understand that it is a sore spot and we can listen to what our feelings want to say about that.

Because a lot of self-development work is learning to be responsible for our own reactions and the effect we are having on those around us, this work is not only important for people who feel fearful or anxious.

With practice you will be able to learn to deal with your stress, anxiety or other negative emotions in a conscious way and avoid pushing them onto other people or acting impulsively.

> Be kind to yourself as you learn to do this. You are not a bad person.

Another important tool for changing less-than-ideal behaviour is, when we know we are feeling triggered, consciously taking a moment to pause and then choosing a different path.

The following exercise is one that you can learn now, but you will have to wait until the next time you feel tempted to act or speak in a way that you do not feel reflects your best self, to use it.

Pause

Allow yourself to stop doing, saying or thinking the thing you know does not reflect you at your best. Stopping mid-sentence, stopping a discussion or action – stopping doing anything that is not positive is always OK.

Within this pause you may need to leave a room, scream into a pillow, write in a journal, exercise or take a few deep breaths. Try to find the most effective way to channel the energy that is used to coming out in a negative way, into a positive, or at least neutral, direction.

Practice, experiment and again - be kind to yourself.

You can do it.

Breathe.

Giving yourself some time is a way of giving yourself the space to be the person you want to be. It is not always easy and it can take a lot of will power, but you will probably find it gets easier the more you practice.

It can also be helpful to accept that part of us wants to be bad, destructive, mean or hard on ourselves. It is a natural counterbalance to our more positive aspects, and to work with that side of us we need to embrace and understand it rather than fight it. As mentioned before, fighting a part of ourselves never goes very well.

For example, when we struggle against an urge we may feel that this is something that has equal power to us, or even power over us. But when we encompass that urge, along with the other aspects of ourselves, with our acceptance we no longer struggle against it as an equal – it is shown to be the smaller part of us that it is. Then, like a strong leader, we can consciously choose the best course of action to take.

We could see this difference in perspective as being "in" the bad feeling, on a level with it and having to struggle with it for power on one hand, or as accepting it as a smaller part of ourselves, while still seeing the big picture and remaining centred and in our integrity on the other.

It might help you to picture the first state as a toddler and the second as an adult. This is not intended as a criticism at all – just a reflection of the fact we can all get knocked into a childish state. And we can all learn to consciously return to our grown-up state.

When you find yourself caught up in a strong feeling or behaving in a way that deep down you know is not right, you can also imagine how it would seem if someone else were acting this way. What would you think of that person? What would others think of them? This can also give you some perspective.

Then, as mentioned before, give yourself some space (even if that means popping to the toilet for 5 minutes) to breathe, centre yourself and come back into your body. Later try to identify what the trigger was and your feelings around it so that you have more choice about how to respond in the future.

You may wonder why in this section we are focusing so much on our actions and the effect it has on those around us. Well, a big part of the reason for doing self-development work is to become a better partner, family member or member of society in general.

But in addition to that, feeling like we have let ourselves down or been bad often leads to more feelings of insecurity, worry or shame (especially if our platform of self-acceptance is already a bit rickety). This in turn can lead to an intensification of feelings of powerlessness, anger, anxiety or other difficult emotions.

So, acceptance and mindful assessment of our behaviour is an opportunity to right the ship and get back on course.

And it is great to prioritise self-control over needing to control external things when trying to make ourselves feel better.

Not uptight, stick-up-your bottom self-control, but a more heart-centred "I clean up after my own emotions" kind of self-control. The kind of self-control you would ask to look after your pet for the weekend.

CHAPTER 6: A LITTLE MORE INFORMATION

This chapter is a random collection of some additional things I think you should know. It will hopefully give you a deeper understanding of negative feelings and how we can sometimes get stuck in them.

If you are feeling any of those emotions quite strongly right now, you might want to focus on using the exercises in the previous chapters and come back to this chapter later on. But if you are feeling fairly OK and grounded, read on.

The Tricky States These Emotions Create

Why can feelings of fear, worry, stress and anxiety be so hard to work with?

Well, there is the obvious point that something that is designed as an alert system should be very loud (and possibly incessant if it feels that the threat is ongoing).

But in addition to that, these emotions all have some qualities that can make them much less fleeting than inspiration or ecstasy.

Feelings of panic or anxiety can create a kind of field of distraction making it hard to focus, as if there was a screen between you and your physical sensations and it was filled with strobe lights, dancing unicorns and clickbait. You feel that you're nearing a grasp of it and then... ..."huh?" (wipes saliva from corner of mouth) or you realise you haven't taken a breath in 10 minutes. This is because fright keeps us out of our physical sensations and deeper thoughts making it hard to concentrate, finish our thoughts or finish anything for that matter.

That's OK, you can accept how you feel and intentionally reconnect with your body and the physical world. Intentionally redirecting some of this nervous energy into physical action or movement can make us feel grounded enough to break its spell.

Worry is similar, but it is more like being on a treadmill that tires us out while strangely also being a comfortable habit. More comfortable for many of us than just relaxing and letting go.

The issue we face with worry is that when we tune into our physical sensations to try and work with it, or when we try and consciously change our thought patterns, the treadmill of repetitive thoughts and worries starts squeaking away again. This often distracts us and puts us in a daze, only to come to a while later and realise that we have slipped into that same old thinking rut again.

If we can accept that that happens, but be mindful of our thoughts, we can learn to consciously take back the reins of our thinking. Changing our physical state will also help shake us out of that "worrying frame of mind" making it a lot harder for worries to sneak back into the captain's chair ("disengage!").

On the other hand, emotions like fear or dread can make us feel leaden and stuck. And although we might feel heavy, this does not mean we are fully present in our bodies. This state is a kind of "heavy frozen", instead of "spacey-frozen" as with panicky feelings. We cannot help but focus on the object of our fear, it weighs on us and we may feel powerless to change our mental, emotional and physical state.

Although you may feel powerless, just go ahead and change your physical state anyway, through exercise, movement and/or breathing. That will give you more room to maneuvre and put things in perspective. You can also get more perspective by talking to a friend or professional, reflecting on the actual reality of the situation or thinking about similar situations that you or others have been in and the best solution.

This has been a very brief overview of the general nature of these feelings, but they may affect you differently. Either way, remember that you have the power to change your state, get help and/ or do something differently.

Letting Old Unhelpful Habits Fall Away

We all have a few thinking and feeling habits that we are used to. However, just because we have become used to something that does not necessarily mean it is right for us.

The culture, family and friends we have been around all shape us in various ways, usually without us thinking about it. In addition, we create some habits for dealing with our emotions and the outside world from a very young age and over time they may become outdated.

It is wise to take a look every so often at the way we habitually feel, think and act and wonder if it reflects our genuine personality and if it is helping us to flourish. Let's look at an example.

Say that a young man grows up amongst people who are very nervous and he has been living a bit of a timid life. He realises that although he also has quite a nervous disposition, he is very creative and wants to take chances with that creativity. So he challenges some of the thinking and behavioural habits he has learned growing up and also begins to channel some of that nervous energy into exercise and into his creativity. His creations reflect a different part of him back to himself and he creates a new self-reinforcing loop - this time a positive one that reinforces his strengths rather than his limitations.

These patterns may involve: thoughts, behaviour, physical tension, emotions or other. They usually affect all aspects of our self, because if one part is affected then they are all affected (even if we think we are good at compartmentalising).

Can you think of a pattern of this sort that may be holding you back?

And do not worry if you cannot see the whole pattern right away. You may just be aware of a habit of thinking negatively about certain things, for example, and not yet know what the emotional and physical aspects of that habit are. That is OK. We only need to spot one recurring or especially challenging thing that is not serving us initially and later the other facets of that may become clear.

If a way of thinking, acting or feeling physically or emotionally does not reflect who you are deep down, you will most likely feel that fact while considering it - this may feel like a sense of unease.

Thinking about Our Patterns

Can you spot any patterns that are not serving your genuine personality?

Do you think they contribute in any way to the stress, fear, anxiety or worry you feel?

Describe the pattern in detail and then I recommend

you allow yourself to acknowledge that this is something that has happened, that that is OK and that you have the strength to change it.

Take a deep breath in and out.

Think about where this pattern may have come from - does someone else you know look, act or feel this way?

If you realise a certain person, group or culture has lead to this pattern in you, allow a sense of acknowledgment and forgiveness to form (as much as feels right to you right now - we often have to forgive in instalments).

Take a deep breath in and out.

And bring the exercise to an end with the knowledge that you have free will and the capacity to change to fulfil your potential

Well done, that can be a tough exercise. And this work is not about blame but understanding, so try to take a kind view towards yourself and others. Everyone is generally doing their best.

Healthy self-development work is a balance between looking at what is not ideal, and just being OK and living our lives. So if you feel that nothing is really wrong, that is great. If you do feel that something is not quite right for you that is also great - you have the opportunity to make a change.

This change should be in line with your personality, at your pace and in the area where it counts. Budging an inch slowly in a difficult area can be a hundred times more effective than leaping into dramatic external action without changing our underlying feelings or thoughts.

And if you have found yourself in the middle of a stressful time, it is worth knowing that pressure, conflict and stress can exacerbate the feeling that something is not working for us, to the point where that thing may become unbearable.

As long as we are taking care of ourselves and we have the capacity to deal with it, this is an excellent opportunity to let go of unnecessary burdens or unhelpful patterns. But if not, just put a pin in it for later.

It feels funny to be writing about patterns here as when I studied Chinese medicine it was all about finding the pattern in what might otherwise seem to be a random collection of symptoms. I suppose that was my first introduction to holistic thought as it applies to people (Tai Chi had already made me see the universe with all the dots joined up).

It is a fun way to think - like we are detectives. Being a detective into our own patterns is a lot harder as it can be difficult to see the forest for the trees. But there are a lot of clues we can look for and they tend be along the lines of: noticing behaviours or words that seem odd or out of proportion, realising we have unexpected or strong feelings, feeling a craving for something, noticing we are self-sabotaging in a particular way or having a reaction to a situation or person that seems unusual.

Thinking about that, do any other possible patterns that you have outgrown come to mind?

Fostering a Way of Being That Suits Us

The phrase *way of being* can be thought of as our "usual state" and it is worth a mention because one of the main issues that people come to me with is that they are living in a state that does not reflect who they are deep down.

Whether this shows up as feeling uneasy, off-centre or uncomfortable in their skin, sleeping poorly or having a lack of concentration or energy, or feeling any of the emotions we have been discussing in this book, for example, the sense of something being "*not quite right*" tends to be at the forefront.

Of course, for some this may stem from an underlying health issue. But when the cause is something else (and often unknown), there are a couple of things that seem to make a big difference and they are connected.

The first is dealing with any unresolved emotional issues - whether that is through counselling or self-reflection and other tools. The other is adopting a lifestyle that suits the person's natural inclinations (including expressing their gifts).

So, if you feel that your negative emotions are at all exacerbated (or even caused) by a way of being that you have outgrown, I recommend you take a big picture look at what that is right now, and what you want it to be.

In the exercise below you are going to put your usual way of being down (on paper, if possible). Although the concept of a *way of being* may sound vague, you can describe emotions, thoughts, habits, behaviours, ways of relating to others, and other things. Also, we are thinking about our usual tendencies, not random or occasional blips. However, if you have felt a certain way for a couple of weeks it is fine to focus on that way of being even if it does not feel natural to you.

Try to avoid value judgements like "good" or "bad", or judging yourself for anything you see as a flaw. Instead focus on words that describe your state, for example: "engaged", "contemplative", "aggravated easily" or "happy when creative", for example. *Way of being* is a big concept, so we will probably end up talking around it, which is more than OK because we want to approach this work as explorers rather than auditors.

Thinking About Our Way of Being

Taking a couple of easy, slow breaths, relax and connect to your body (you can use one of the methods from earlier in the book if that helps).

Just notice how you are feeling and create a sense of open-minded curiosity, like a child's.

Now write out how you generally feel and act in terms of mood, energy levels, creativity, joy, physicality, thinking habits, relating to others, taking chances, expressing yourself and having fun. Also think about how you are: at home, at work, with family and with friends if any of these are different.

Finally, how would you say other people see you?

Take a moment to feel good about being open and exploring this topic with little or no judgement.

Your best way of being is solely up to you, it cannot really be usefully compared to other peoples', because its purpose is to house and support your unique personality.

The only time comparison may be slightly helpful is if we feel a twinge of envy and when looking into that we realise that someone is doing something we want to do (and that can be anything from self-care to podcasts to aerial dance to an MBA). Then we can draw our line of sight back to our own future and work towards something that a part of us is aching to express.

So, ideally we will work towards the way of being that feels natural to us, reflects our genuine personality and is healthy and balanced. This may feel like halfway between you on a holiday you're enjoying, and you when engaged in something that you are excited and actively engaged by (such as work, a hobby or other).

It is not about total relaxation, perfection, or never being stressed – it is a healthy state of being centred in yourself, grounded in your body, connected to reality, breathing, engaged or relaxed (as appropriate), self-compassionate, connected to others, awake (not in terms of sleeping, but attitude), aware and able to grow and evolve.

And it will most likely help your feelings of fear, stress, worry or anxiety because a grounded, genuine and embodied way of being is very different from the breathless whirlwind of anxiety or the rigidity of fear.

Of course we all get knocked off-course sometimes and occasionally life has plans that are bigger than our wellbeing needs. At these times I recommend you try the exercises you have learned in this book to get more grounded in your body and work through your feelings. Also, always stay open to asking for professional help if you need it.

One Last Exercise

I love this exercise, but it is not for people who are in the middle of strong emotions or feelings of fear or anxiety, which is why I have kept it for last. If you are feeling fairly centred right now you can try it. On the other hand, if you do not feel you can deal with any extra emotion right now come back to this later instead.

This is great for releasing patterns of tension from inside our torso. These are often associated with certain feelings or held emotion, so shifting them can lead to an emotional release or a change in our general physical and emotional state. If you feel emotions coming up you can work through them using an exercise from chapter 3. Or you can also take a break and then try again later.

Massaging the Inside of Our Body with Our Breath

Having released some of the more obvious tension in your body, we can now work into some deeper areas of tension, which can often be hard to reach.

Without causing any pain or over-breathing (hyperventilating) at all, we are going to use our breathing to reach some of these places.

It may feel strange to create more space in areas that have not felt spacious for a long time, but as long as it doesn't hurt it is fine.

> Sit or lie comfortably and close your eyes.

> Put your hands on your belly and feel them moving out as you push your belly out to breathe in

> As you keep breathing in and out deeply and slowly, increase the distance your abdomen extends with each in-breath. Feel it stretching your abdomen outwards. Do not arch your back.

> Now, as you continue to do that, include your upper abdomen in that movement. This is the area in the centre line of your body under your rib cage. If it helps, move your hands up to that area and push them out as you breathe in.

> After a couple of breaths pushing your upper abdomen out, put your hands on your chest and push them up and out with your in-breath. See if you can also move your hands away from each other by expanding your ribcage as you breathe in

> Now with your hands on each side of your torso, on your lower ribs, breathe to push your hands apart sideways

> You can now go on to breathe into any area you feel is restricted for a few breaths, changing the area as

needed (without causing any pain). Possible areas include: the top of your shoulders, the inside of your shoulder blades, between your shoulder blades, the middle or lower back, deeper into your pelvis, and any other area that feels like it needs more space or movement, as long as it does not cause pain.

You can do this for as long as it is comfortable, up to a maximum of 10 minutes.

When you are ready to stop, place your hands on your legs and take a moment to enjoy the feeling of spaciousness you have created. Slowly open your eyes.

Did you notice that a certain area had a lot more/less movement or tension than you expected? This exercise is interesting because many of us only think of working with the muscles on the outside of our body when we picture getting a massage.

However, since our bodies are designed to work the best when we move throughout the day (and this varied movement massages them inside) supplementing that internal movement sometimes can be useful - both in terms of maintaining a good physical state, and for moving stuck emotions.

Fearful States vs Genuine Living

As I briefly mentioned above, I have noticed that a sense of unexpressed potential often crops up alongside fearful and anxious states. I feel that if we have an ability, something to say or something we want to make that we are not using, saying or creating, the pressure of holding it in can build up inside us, leading to panicky feelings and fears.

Of course this is a bit of a chicken and egg situation - it is hard to know whether people experiencing fear or worry tend not to not leave their comfort zone, or if it is the not leaving of the comfort zone that causes the fearful feelings. But I think it is a cycle, one that we may be able to break by pushing ourselves to grow. Evolution is a natural part of life, so if you have an aspect of yourself that you would like to explore I urge you to try it.

And this does not have to be a death-defying leap into a new career, it can be dipping half your little toe in to test the water. Sometimes people who do not realise they are scared (of change, failure or success, for example) will throw themselves into something in such a way that it is more likely to fail. Also, lurching into scary action, although sometimes appropriate, may lead to a disconnect with our bodies.

So you can be sensible, accept your fear, anxiety, worry or resistance, and edge forward in such a way that you can stay fully embodied. Take sustainable steps, breathe, forgive yourself when you make the mistakes that are essential for learning and progress, and discover and enjoy new parts of yourself.

It is interesting to consider that not only can other emotions be shunted into feelings of fear and anxiety – so can the latent power of our potential.

CONCLUSION

I hope this short and slightly eclectic guide has helped you a little. The weaknesses and flaws we have, we will always have - but it is worth bearing in mind that our strength, self-love and adaptability can grow to encompass and outweigh them.

And it is also worth knowing that within every weakness is a strength, if handled appropriately. For example, our anxiety may be related to artistic sensitivity, fear may lead to insight and preparation, worry may tell us what we care about. None of these things should have the reins, but all can be valuable in their own way.

If you want to get in touch feel free to email me at hello@suzannewylde.com (please include the book title in the subject line, it helps me!). Also, if this book helped you, it would be very kind if you could take the time to leave a review so others know it can help them too.

My internet things are: @suzanne_wylde on Instagram, @Wyldesuzanne on Facebook and a website: www.suzannewylde.com which has more self-help tools and information.

As a special thank you for buying this book, I have created some additional resources that you can find here: https://www.suzannewylde.com/happy-andstrong.

Also, if you think this book might help a friend of yours please let them know. It would be great if this can reach the people who need it right now.

I'd like to leave you with a quote that reminds us of the importance of having fun and enjoying life even though experiences of adversity, challenge or failure are inevitable:

> *"I am going to keep having fun every day I have left, because there is no other way of life. You just have to decide whether you are a Tigger or an Eeyore."*
>
> – Randy Pausch

APPENDIX: THE EXERCISES

Exercises for Body Connection

<u>Big Yawn and Stretch</u>

Have a big yawn and stretch. Now exaggerate it, open your mouth really wide and make a sound as you sigh or yawn loudly. Repeat this as you move your body a little more in the way that feels good to you.

Coming Back into Your Body

As you do this exercise either choose the option that applies to you the most or make another one up that feels true. Also, try to look either straight ahead or down, but not up.

Put your hands on your belly.

Look down at your body and say "hello body, thank you for _____ [moving me around/ making life enjoyable/ working hard/ digesting all my food/ keeping me going/ storing all my feelings and other aspects of me]. I love you, thank you".

Now rub your hands up and down your thighs strongly, bringing your awareness into the feeling in your legs.

Wiggle your toes and circle your feet around, bringing that awareness into your lower legs also.

When you feel that you are very connected to your legs, expand that awareness from your legs through your hips and then to your whole torso and your arms. As you do this you can also move and breathe in the way you feel your body wants to in order to get that awareness everywhere in your body (safely and without pain) for as long as you feel like. Groaning or yawning noises may help.

What does it feel like to be more connected to your body right now?

Stay with this feeling as you take a deep breath in and out

See if you can feel this feeling even more fully as you take another breath in and out

Foot Massage for Feeling Safe and Relaxed

There is almost nothing that signals "I am not in danger" to our bodies, hearts and minds than taking the time to massage our feet.

So pop one foot up and gently work into those muscles. You can also circle your foot around and then gently stretch your toes back and forth with your hands.

Without causing any pain, increase the firmness so you are releasing tension you do not need, but in a smooth and flowing way so your feet feel reassured (yes, feet can feel reassured).

Take a deep, slow and relaxing breath, yawn and stretch if you feel like it.

Exercises for Accepting Ourselves and Our Feelings

<u>Taking a Moment to Fully Recognise How Well You Are Doing</u>

In this exercise we are going to say a short phrase to ourselves to acknowledge our worth and to feel self-acceptance and self-love. If the phrase seems too much or wrong you can change it – as long as it is still positive.

Close your eyes, breathe deeply and in a relaxed way

Let a feeling of warmth and love grow in your chest and spread throughout your body. Say to yourself "I am good, I am strong, I am enough" and breathe in and out slowly and deeply

If anything comes up to block that, just accept that part of you, whilst also knowing you can feel a level of self-love and self-acceptance at the same time – there is space for both within you.

Repeat the phrase "I am good, I am strong, I am enough" the number of times that feels right

Let the feeling of warmth, self-acceptance and self-love move around your body anywhere it is needed. It can even encompass difficult emotions or areas of your body you have a hard time loving.

When you are ready to end the exercise take a deep breath in and out and open your eyes.

Accepting my Body

Take a deep breath in and out slowly.

Put your hands on your body wherever you like – chest, shoulders, stomach, legs.

Say in your mind or aloud "this is my perfect body" (and if you feel that your body is not perfect right now for some reason add the phrase "thank you for doing your best for me".)

If that is hard, just accept the feeling of it being hard and feel good about your effort, then try it again.

Take another deep breath in and out.

Great job embodied person, and great tummy!

Taking a Moment to Remember That We're Only Human

Sit comfortably, put your hands on your heart, belly or on your legs, take a deep breath in and say "I accept that I'm only human and I am doing the best I can"

Say it a few times if you want to, and after each time breathe in and feel that you are breathing in self-acceptance.

Be with the stillness that arises

Accepting a Wide Range of Emotions

Take a slow and relaxing breath in and out.

Be aware of your physical sensations
and accept anything you feel.

Going at your own pace, call to mind each of
the emotions below one at a time and feel your
acceptance of that emotion in your body. If it helps
you can think or say "I accept feeling ___" for each.

If you find it hard to accept any, that is OK,
just accept the resistance and move on.

*Happy, annoyed, angry, weak, powerful, wrong,
embarrassed, anxious, excited, afraid, satisfied,
insecure, out-of-control, empowered*

Take a deep breath in and out

Exercises for Processing Emotions

<u>Connecting to Our Physical Sensations</u>

(For this exercise only look straight ahead or down – not up)

Go ahead and rub your thighs quite firmly again.

Have a move around of your body.

Have a yawn and a loud sigh.

Now pause and notice how your body is feeling. Are there any sensations at the forefront?

Focus on the most noticeable feeling (or even absence of feeling, like numbness)

Describe it to yourself, possibly including temperature, colour, shape, feelings of heaviness/lightness or movement. Get as specific as you can.

When you have a complete picture in your mind, just put a pin in it for now and taking a deep breath, open your eyes.

Connecting to Our Emotions and Working with Them

Bring yourself fully into your body again by rubbing your thighs, moving about a bit and breathing deeply and slowly (while still looking only ahead or down – not up).

Focus your awareness on your body and notice the most obvious physical sensation. Just be aware of it for a moment, without any need to do anything.

Holding it gently in your awareness, let a picture form as if it was a representation of the feeling. Allow all the details to appear including its: shape, colour, temperature, texture or movement if any.

Once you have that pictured clearly in your mind, say "hello" to it and just be with it for a moment without expectation.

Then, when you feel ready, ask it if it has anything it wants to say and wait for the answer with an open mind. There are no wrong answers, but we don't want our mind to step in and supply the answer, so try and just wait until something organically pops up.

If it answered you there is a chance that you could have a dialogue back and forth, so you can try that. If it did not answer you, you may want to repeat the exercise at a later time.

Either way you can also try asking "is there anything you want?"

If it answers, you can either have a dialogue with it, or just acknowledge its feelings.

When you feel that the conversation or interaction is complete you can either end the exercise or you can repeat it with another noticeable physical sensation.

Exercise for Grounded Thinking

How Realistic Are Our Thoughts?

If you have specific worries, negative repetitive thoughts, stories or beliefs associated with your feelings of fear or anxiety, identify one or two and then examine them thoroughly using the following questions. Also try not to answer any reflexively, but take your time.

1. Is it absolutely true?
2. Would most other people agree with that thought or belief?
3. Is it in proportion? (e.g., being as terrified of making a spelling mistake as falling from a great height is out of proportion – even if you are a perfectionist)
4. If it is about yourself or another person, is it the most honest and loving it can be? Or is it unnecessarily harsh or critical?

If you have found that the thing or things you are thinking are not the most realistic, create the most real version of them and write that down.

How does thinking the most realistic version of the thought feel?

Exercises for When the Way We Behaved Was Outside our Integrity

<u>Accepting We Behaved Poorly</u>

Write the sentence that sums up your behaviour the most accurately, choosing the right words for you, (they can be different to the examples given below):

"I accept that I was _____ rude/ short/ passive aggressive/ critical/ stubborn/ angry because I felt _____ stressed/ afraid/ disrespected/ insecure/ unloved/ anxious".

With your hands on your heart, say in your mind or aloud:
"I accept that sometimes I get _____ when I feel _____"

Breathe in acceptance of that statement

Breath out with a wide open mouth letting go of any need to be perfect

Breathe in self-acceptance deeply

Breathe out with a wide open mouth letting go of self-imposed pressure

(repeat until you feel finished)

Pause

Allow yourself to stop doing, saying or thinking the thing you know does not reflect you at your best. Stopping mid-sentence, stopping a discussion or action – stopping doing anything that is not positive is always OK.

Within this pause you may need to leave a room, scream into a pillow, write in a journal, exercise or take a few deep breaths. Try to find the most effective way to channel the energy that is used to coming out in a negative way, into a positive, or at least neutral, direction.

Practice, experiment and again - be kind to yourself.

You can do it.

Breathe.

Exercises for Looking at Our Patterns and Way of Being

Thinking About Our Patterns

Can you spot any patterns that are not serving your genuine personality?

Do you think they contribute in any way to the stress, fear, anxiety or worry you feel?

Describe the pattern in detail and then I recommend you allow yourself to acknowledge that this is something that has happened, that that is OK and that you have the strength to change it.

Take a deep breath in and out.

Think about where this pattern may have come from (does someone else you know look, act or feel this way?).

If you realise a certain person, group or culture has lead to this pattern in you, allow a sense of acknowledgment and forgiveness to form (as much as feels right to you right now - we often have to forgive in instalments)

Take a deep breath in and out.

And bring the exercise to an end with the knowledge that you have free will and the capacity to change to fulfil your potential

Thinking About Our Way of Being

Taking a couple of easy, slow breaths, relax and connect to your body (you can use one of the methods from earlier in the book if that helps).

Just notice how you are feeling and create a sense of open-minded curiosity - like a child's.

Now write out how you generally are in terms of mood, energy levels, creativity, joy, physicality, thinking habits, relating to others, taking chances, expressing yourself and having fun. Also think about how you are: at home, at work, with family and with friends if any of these are different.

Finally, how would you say other people see you?

Take a moment to feel good about being open and exploring this topic with little or no judgement.

An Exercise for Deeper Relaxation (for When We Are Feeling Pretty Good Already)

Massaging the Inside of Our Body With Our Breath

Having released some of the more obvious tension in your body, we can now work into some deeper areas of tension, which can often be hard to reach.

Without causing any pain or over-breathing (hyperventilating) at all, we are going to use our breathing to reach some of these places.

It may feel strange to create more space in areas that have not felt spacious for a long time, but as long as it doesn't hurt it is fine.

> Sit or lie comfortably and close your eyes.
>
> Put your hands on your belly and feel them moving out as you push your belly out to breathe in
>
> As you keep breathing in and out deeply and slowly, increase the distance your abdomen extends each time. Feel it stretching your abdomen outwards. Do not arch your back.
>
> Now as you continue to do that, include your upper abdomen in that movement. This is the area in the centre line of your body under your rib cage. If it helps, move your hands up to that area and push them out as you breathe.

After a couple of breaths pushing your upper
abdomen out, put your hands on your chest and
push them up and out with your breath. See if
you can also move them away from each other
by expanding your ribcage as you breathe

Now with your hands on each side of your torso, on
your lower ribs, breathe to push your hands apart
sideways

You can now go on to breathe into any area you feel
is restricted for a few breaths, changing the area as
needed (without causing any pain). Possible areas
include: the top of your shoulders, the inside of your
shoulder blades, between your shoulder blades, the
middle or lower back, deeper into your pelvis, and
any other area that feels like it needs more space
or movement, as long as it does not cause pain.

You can do this for as long as is comfortable,
up to a maximum of 10 minutes.

When you are ready to stop, place your
hands on your legs and take a moment to
enjoy the feeling of spaciousness you have
created. Slowly open your eyes.

PRAISE FOR AUTHOR

"I recommend [Suzanne] in a heartbeat. One of the most powerful sessions I have ever experienced. I had the feeling she connected to my soul and reflected the messages I needed to hear with insight and care. She intuitively guided me to integrate what was needed for me to leave the session feeling physically and mentally lighter and at peace with-in. Don't think twice, book your session."

- NICOLA MOSS

I have come so far since first meeting Suzanne, and my journey continues. I am constantly looking back, with a smile on my face, at how far I keep coming....

Stay curious, and let Suzanne guide you gently through your own journey. Believe me, you will only ever look back to smile at the journey you too have made xx."

- SUSAN M, LONDON

BOOKS BY THIS AUTHOR

Moving Stretch: Work Your Fascia To Free Your Body

Moving Stretch is a powerful and enjoyable type of stretching that not only strengthens and frees the body, but reconditions the body's fascia, rejuvenates the tissue, releases adhesions, relieves pain, and increases flexibility.

This accessible guide gives step-by-step instructions for people who are tight and inflexible, those with poor posture, athletes who want to boost their performance, and those who want something more than conventional stretching.

Resistance stretching works on the fascia that makes us the shape we are, so it is a powerful technique. Even just 10-20 minutes of stretching a day can make a big difference!

This is the UK version, see below for Canada and the US.

Moving Stretch: Work Your Fascia To Free Your Body

The US version of this book has a different cover but the same great content. Moving Stretch has been helping thousands of people in North America improve their mobility, flexibility and strength, with great results.

The Art Of Coming Home

This easy-to-read self-development guide uses practical, common-sense principles, visualisations and thought-provoking advice to teach you to connect to your own innate wisdom to become your own guru.

Combining tools created for her clients from experience, tried and tested advice and academic research, Suzanne covers topics such as; building self-love and self-compassion, finding your own inner wisdom, learning to process your emotions and connect to your body, expand your way of thinking, become more conscious and connect to the aspects of yourself from the past.

This book will support you in learning to access and

appreciate the full value and potential of your authentic self.

This title will be released in July 2020.

www.ingramcontent.com/pod-product-compliance
Lightning Source LLC
Chambersburg PA
CBHW071750080526
44588CB00013B/2204